Is the Loch Ness Monster Real?

BY ALLISON LASSIEUR

AMICUS HIGH INTEREST ❖ AMICUS INK

Amicus High Interest and Amicus Ink are imprints of Amicus
P.O. Box 1329, Mankato, MN 56002
www.amicuspublishing.us

Library of Congress Cataloging-in-Publication Data
Lassieur, Allison, author.
 Is the Loch Ness Monster real? / by Allison Lassieur.
     pages cm. – (Amicus high interest) (Unexplained. What's
the evidence?)
 Summary: "Presents stories of the Loch Ness monster in
Scotland, examining the evidence of various explanations and
hoaxes surrounding this legend"– Provided by publisher.
 Audience: K to grade 3.
 Includes index.
 ISBN 978-1-60753-805-9 (library binding) –
 ISBN 978-1-60753-894-3 (ebook)
 ISBN 978-1-68152-046-9 (paperback)
1. Loch Ness monster–Juvenile literature. 2. Legends–Scotland–
Juvenile literature. I. Title.
 QL89.2.L6L37 2016
 001.944–dc23
                                                    2014038740

Series Editor   Rebecca Glaser
Series Designer   Kathleen Petelinsek
Book Designer   Heather Dreisbach
Photo Researcher   Derek Brown

Photo Credits:
Science Photo Library/Alamy, Cover; Circumnavigation/
Shutterstock, 5; Victor Habbick/Shutterstock, 6; Antonino
Barbagallo/Corbis, 9; Peter J. Hatcher/Alamy, 10; Mary
Evans Picture Library/Alamy, 13; R. K. Wilson/Fortean Picture
Library, 14; Ian Tyas/Stringer/Getty Images, 17; Tim Dinsdale/
Dinsdale Family, 18; Anton_Ivanov/Shutterstock, 21; Cascade
News Ltd./Splash News/Corbis, 22; Michael Rosskothen/
Shutterstock, 25; Dung Vo Trung/Sygma/Corbis, 26; Kletr/
Shutterstock, 29

Printed in North Mankato, Minnesota

HC 10 9 8 7 6 5 4 3 2
PB 10 9 8 7 6 5 4 3 2 1

Table of Contents

What Is the Loch Ness Monster?

In Scotland, there is a famous lake called Loch Ness. It is about 23 miles (37 km) long. It is 1 mile (1.6 km) wide. It is very deep. Loch Ness holds more water than any other lake in Scotland. A river flows from the lake to the sea. Some people believe a huge creature lives in the lake. They call it the Loch Ness monster.

 What is a loch?

Loch Ness is a beautiful
lake in Scotland.

 Loch is the Scottish word for "lake."

This is one artist's idea of what the Loch Ness monster looks like.

 Does the Loch Ness monster have a nickname?

6

No one knows for sure how big the monster is. Some say it has a long neck. It uses flippers to swim. There are humps on its back. The monster swims fast through the water. Sometimes it comes to the surface of the water. That is when people see the monster. Or so the stories say.

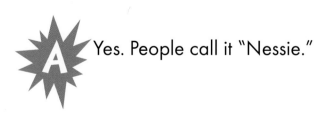

Yes. People call it "Nessie."

7

Around the world, there are many reports of strange monsters. A few people claim to have seen them. One or two blurry photos may make us wonder. But there are thousands of reports about the Loch Ness monster. If so many people have seen it, is it true? The photos are not clear. No one knows for sure what could be in the lake.

A picture like this does not prove there is a monster in the lake. It could be fake.

9

More than 1,400 years ago, St. Columba said he saw a monster in the Ness River.

First Reports

The legend of the Loch Ness monster is more than 1,400 years old. The oldest story is about a **monk** at Loch Ness. He heard about a monster. It lived in a river near the lake. The monk went to the river. He saw the monster. The monster saw him and sank into the water.

Over time, other people said they saw the monster. Their reports did not get much attention. In 1933, a new road was built around the lake. The road had clear views of the water. One day a couple saw a monster from the road! A newspaper wrote about it. The news spread. This time, the world found out about Nessie.

Many people tried to spot Nessie after a news story in 1933.

A doctor took this picture at Loch Ness in 1934.

 Many people do not believe in monsters. Why did people think the surgeon's photo was real?

14

Monster hunters went to the lake. But they did not spot Nessie. In 1934, Dr. Robert Wilson brought a picture of an animal to a newspaper. The animal had a long neck. It was swimming in a lake. He said it was the Loch Ness monster. The picture was known as the "**surgeon**'s photo." It made Nessie famous!

 Everyone thought a doctor would tell the truth.

15

Loch Ness Monster Sightings

The hunt for Nessie was on! People who lived near the lake told stories of seeing the monster. People from around the world went to Loch Ness. They hoped to see Nessie. Hundreds of people reported seeing the monster. Some people saw a large hump in the water. It moved fast. Some people said it looked like an overturned boat.

A team of people kept watch in 1969. They hoped to catch Nessie on film.

17

Tim Dinsdale spent much of his life looking for the Loch Ness monster.

 Did Tim Dinsdale believe he saw a monster?

Some of the **witnesses** took pictures. They showed a large, dark hump in the water. In 1960, Tim Dinsdale took a video. It showed an object moving in the water. He was sure it was the Loch Ness monster. Since then, many others have made videos. The videos show *something* moving in the water. But what was it?

 Yes. He quit his job as an engineer to look for the monster full time. He spent the rest of his life searching for Nessie.

Exposing the Fakes

Most of the Loch Ness monster stories are **hoaxes**. The biggest hoax was the surgeon's photo. The monster was made out of a toy. But people did not find out until 60 years later!

In 1972, a man pulled a body out of Loch Ness. It turned out to be a dead seal. A man had put it there as a joke.

 Why do people make up hoaxes?

20

Seals and other sea creatures can look like monsters from far away.

A For many reasons. Maybe they think it would be a fun joke. Or they want to be famous.

21

22

In 2012, a boat captain named George Edwards took the "best ever" picture of the monster. It showed Nessie's hump. But a year later, Edwards told the truth. The hump was a **prop**. It was used for a TV show about the monster. Edwards said he did it to have some fun.

George Edwards took this picture. He said it was the Loch Ness monster. Many people believed him at first.

What's the Evidence?

If there is a monster in Loch Ness, what is it? One idea is that it is a **plesiosaur**. These water reptiles lived millions of years ago, at the time of dinosaurs. The loch is big enough. But plesiosaurs breathed air. They would be on the surface a lot. They also need a lot of food. There isn't much food in the loch.

Plesiosaurs lived millions of years ago.

25

Boaters hope to see Nessie, but Loch Ness is huge.

 Q What was the biggest Loch Ness expedition?

So what proof is there? Not much. A few big **expeditions** have tried to find the monster. They use **sonar** to look underwater and take pictures. One picture shows a large animal with a long neck. Another photo shows a cave where Nessie might hide. But the pictures are often not clear. People guess what they are seeing.

 Operation Deepscan studied the lake in 1987. Sonar showed a large moving object. No one knows what it was.

Many people say they see large humps in the water. The humps could be from a **sturgeon**. Sturgeons are huge ocean fish. They only come to fresh water to lay eggs. This would explain why Nessie is not seen much. It also explains how Nessie could still be around after all this time. If there really is something in Loch Ness, that is.

Sturgeon can grow as big as sharks.

Glossary

expedition A journey by a group of people for a specific purpose, such as research or exploration.

hoax A trick or joke in which someone tries to make people believe something is real, but it is not.

monk A man who is a part of a religious group.

plesiosaur A water reptile with a long neck, flippers, and a short tail.

prop An item used in a play or show to make the audience believe the story.

sonar A device that can find objects deep underwater using sound waves.

sturgeon A large ocean fish.

surgeon A doctor who performs operations.

witness A person who saw or heard something firsthand.

Read More

Karst, Ken. *Loch Ness Monster.* Mankato, Minn.: Creative Education, 2014.

Rivkin, Jennifer. *Searching for the Loch Ness Monster.* New York: PowerKids Press, 2015.

Schach, David. *The Loch Ness Monster.* Minneapolis: Bellwether Media, 2011.

Sievert, Terri. *The Unsolved Mystery of the Loch Ness Monster.* North Mankato, Minn.: Capstone Press, 2013.

Websites

Fact Monster: The Loch Ness Monster
www.factmonster.com/biography/var/lochnessmonster.html

Loch Ness and Inverness: Discover and Explore
www.visitlochness.com/kids/index.html

PBS: NOVA: The Beast of Loch Ness
www.pbs.org/wgbh/nova/lochness/

Every effort has been made to ensure that these websites are appropriate for children. However, because of the nature of the Internet, it is impossible to guarantee that these sites will remain active indefinitely or that their contents will not be altered.

31

Index

About the Author

Allison Lassieur loves reading and writing about strange, mysterious, and unusual places in the world. She has written more than 150 books for kids, and she also likes to write about history, food, and science. Allison lives in a house in the woods with her husband, daughter, three dogs, two cats, and a blue fish named Marmalade.